C000253373

OSTRICH™

Ostrich Publishers

Made in the U.S.A

www.ostrichpress.com

# The Telesales Handbook

OSTRICH ™

Ostrich Publishers

Made in the U.S.A

www.ostrichpress.com

**Ostrich Publishers**

*Charlotte, NC 28212*

ISBN: 9781673465327

For more information about products and services or perhaps to make additional purchases, visit our official website at www.ostrichpress.com. We look forward to producing and /or publishing more books in the future. You can also visit Amazon.com or anywhere books are sold to purchase any of our other works.

While the author has made every effort to provide accurate telephone numbers, internet addresses, and other contact information at the time of publication of this book, neither the publisher nor the author assumes any responsibility for errors or for changes that occur after publication. In addition, the author assumes no responsibility for the accuracy of any information presented here in this book.

# OSTRICH PUBLISHERS

www.ostrichpress.com

# THE
# TELESALES
# HANDBOOK

## Learn How to Sell Anything
## Over the Phone

## FRANK DAPPAH

*Co-Founder of Corvus Web Services*
*www.corvus.website*

For Bernice, my partner, biggest fan, my love, and the hardest working salesperson I know.

Thanks for laughing at my strange jokes and enduring my many pointless rants and uninformed opinions.

# THE BIG KAHUNA

*"We became masters of all we survey via a set of unique intellectually inspired manifestations, actions, proclivities and projections the still drive our mere existence and commerce today"*

Did you know that according to the Fossil record, we humans are among the last species to show up on the face of the earth? Yes, we are. Trippy, right?

The Dinosaurs, Plesiosaurs, even the common Turtle, were here before we got here.

Even land-dwelling mammals like the Pakicetus (Ancestors of certain Whale and Dolphin species) become marine animals long before we showed up.

Our first known ancestor is thought to have walked the earth some five million to seven million years ago. And yet Homosapiens (Initially of the Hominidae order) quickly climbed the food chain. It did not take us long to crown ourselves the big Kahunas of the animal kingdom.

Today, we (Humans) dominate every corner of the globe. We seem to, with extreme efficiency, either eradicate or subjugate other life forms everywhere we go.

We have no natural predators. Our success as a species stems not from some natural ability to defend ourselves against those who would want to make dinner out of us, but rather our intelligence, gumption, wit. Unlike the Lion, or say the wolf, we do not have a heightened sense of smell or sight.

We do not possess the ability to run fast or any other natural visible advantageous adaptation. We have had to, or rather our brains have had to evolve into this marvelous piece of equipment with which we have and continue to advance beyond any other known species on earth.

You get the picture. Yes, our brains, and more specifically, our ability to use our noggins to find ways to coordinate with one another is what makes us earth's dominant species.

## *We are great communicators*

Those that rule one place we have left untouched - the seas, function very much the same way.

Killer whales or Orcas, the ocean's badasses have a similar ability to communicate with freakish precision and work together to take down prey 10x the size of each individual. Communication is what we do.

This is how we built our cities, discovered new planets, found cures for diseases, even worked to try to find the meaning of our very existence. No other creature is aware of their own being and works hard, with others to make their lives better. We do! This is who we are.

## *Effervescence of our Humanity*

In business, more specifically, sales, you will have to lean on these astonishing qualities to help you prevail.

Financial Advisors and Money managers must look to their ability to succinctly communicate their various investment strategies and work closely with their clients to deliver results in-line with the needs and wants of each client.

Those in the creative arts, even more than the rest of us must reach deep into the abyss of their very souls to create works that speak directly to us. These creations, the ones folks like Jean Michel Basquiat created speak to us even today.

Even after some 30 years later, those vivid red graffiti-like works of art still speak to us.

Healthcare professionals must spend all day connecting and reaching folks, not just with their healing hands but with words of kindness and reassurance.

Words that are often desperately needed for afflicted souls and those that love them to look forward to another day.

Empathy and eloquence and compassion and honesty are just of the tools needed to win at life and business.

## *Groups - tribes*

*It is easy to forget that not so long ago, our ancestors roamed the wild.*

From the plains of Africa to the caves of what is now the Middle East, earlier humans had to wake up every day and deal with the same hardships other species still deal with today.

Most creatures in the wild have to constantly fend-off predators while navigating the everyday life stuff of a living organism - Reproduction, feeding etc.

Not only did we roam the wild at the same time as the Mastodon, but we put him and others like him on our dinner menu.

There have been numerous discoveries of the remains of some of these giant ancient creatures found with man-made weapons lodged in their carcasses.

Back in 1977, archaeologist Carl Gustafson – then at Washington State University in Pullman – excavated a male mastodon near Sequim, Washington. Buried in one of the ribs he found a bone fragment that didn't belong to the elephant-like animal, which he suggested was from the tip of a weapon used to kill the beast. We took down some really formidable creatures in our earlier days.

So how did we do this? We worked together. Now you may not realize this, but we are pack creatures.

Smaller groups grew to become tribes, tribes to countries and so on. Even today, if you look at the political climate in this country and others, man's need to band together, and fight others is still very much part of us.

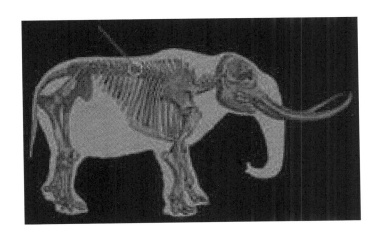

The location of the rib and approximate angle of the spear, which had to penetrate 25 to 30 centimeters of hide, tissue and bone (Image: Center for the Study of the First Americans, Texas A&M University)

### *The power of us*

Let's face it!

Our need to connect for a common good oftentimes goes far beyond just the tasks on which we embark. We (Humans) tend to be very competitive as well. We, in both commercial and private instances place value on things as it relates to the others' view, need or want for it.

This inexplicable phenomenon is typically on full display in fashion, art, and in general business parlance.

Business folks talk a lot about " The Competition".

We evaluate the performance and value of our companies based on how they stack up to similar organizations and the broader markets.

As businesspersons and sales folk, we use this inalienable feature of humanity in various ways. We are able to evaluate the market demand for our products and services and create marketing strategies around the general, infectious reception of our offerings.

We are able to build demand models around how receptive our ideas are to a group of people with common views, issues, needs, etc.

The whole idea of social media and social media marketing, from the perspective of the organizations that seek to capitalize on our behavior online is built on this idea.

The idea that we like to behave like [Us] and most of us will develop an affinity for products and services based on how popular said offerings are among our friends, colleagues, and family members. Us.

# WHAT TO EXPECT

*Telesales, Over-the-phone sales or selling products and services over the phone can help bring untold profits to your business.*

The idea of calling folks up and asking if they want to buy something may seem strange in this modern age of social media and mobile apps. A time when we all seem to be so far removed from one another.

I always thought the introduction of all these gizmos and platforms was supposed to make us " more connected".

The thing is, nothing could be further

from the truth. The youth today, around the world, now have to deal with issues never thought conceivable at such young ages. For instance, a 2018 report from Blue Cross Blue Shield found that diagnoses of major depression had risen 47 percent for millennials in 2013.

In fact, despite all the advancements we have made to help humans connect more with one another, a key ingredient in productivity, we all seem to be drifting apart.

Most of us spend most of our online browsing time not engaging in substantive productive interactions but rather on petty stuff. Mob-like behavior has now become a substitute for social activism. I long for the day we can all go back to engaging in the kind of dialogue that inspires, educates, or at the very least help move our species forward in some meaningful way.

## *A Well-defined Audience*

According to numerous studies by the Pew Research Institute, a significant number of young adults and Millennials consider online interactions as being "Social".

Looking at these trends, it is easy for you to assume that the idea of selling over the phone is an impossibility.

But keep in mind that older individuals and businesses still make a lot of their buying decisions as a result of a phone conversation. So, although the prospect of selling stuff over the phone to younger, savvier folks may seem less straightforward than in recent times, there is still great opportunity in marketing to older cohorts and B2B folks.

### Three main ideas

*The general idea(s) behind this book can be split into three main sections.*

In this book "The Telesales Handbook", a second in my series of Handbooks, the first being "The Social Media Marketing Handbook, I will try to drive home three main ideas. The idea that telesales or phone sales is still alive and well, and that other well-known firms are currently making a whole bunch of money by investing in phone sales teams. I will also try to share my thoughts on which products, in my experience are great for phone sales.

These will be the kinds of software applications, tools, and platforms that will help facilitate a smooth transition for you and/or your team into the exciting world of telesales. Now, I am certain, there will be, and you can think of many other products and service categories to add to this list. I have no doubt about that!

Please keep in mind that this is just my opinion on the subject matter. I am by no means making the assertion that any list of products and/or tools I provide will be a "complete" one.

In this book, I will also share some call scripts out there that I have used or examined and think will be of great value to you as a starting point to help develop your own custom scripts. Ones that will certainly be unique to you, your firm, and the products and services you sell.

You can expect during this book that I will use a lot of technical terms to illustrate various thought processes, techniques, and processes. Let me apologize in advance. I am merely an entrepreneur with zero artistic acumen.

I will try to share my experiences to the best of my literary abilities. In this book, I am looking to talk to any entrepreneur or solo salesperson out there thinking about venturing into a new product category or perhaps looking for new ways to market an existing product line.

This book would be of great value to you. Especially if you sell insurance or financial products, telecommunication or information technology services, Web design and software development products, and so on.

*Great! Let's get started*

# THE TELESALES HANDBOOK

## CONTENTS

# ⇄ CHAPTER ONE⇄

# A COMPELLING CASE

## *Sales is highly customizable!*

The greatest difference between sales and marketing, in my humble opinion, is that while marketing seeks to attract a group of well-defined cohorts to buy into an idea with a fairly rigid message, sales, on the other hand, employs a more hands-on approach.

Salespeople, for better or worse are extreme evangelists of the products and services we sell. Sales is highly customizable. well, the messaging is. For example, I could sell a product, the same type of, let's say insurance to both an older woman and a young lady. Although each would be examining the viability of the same product.

My technique, tone, and the features I decided to highlight will differ for both women. That is the magic of sales. It is personal, it is human, it's made to suit. You can sell anything.

Selling over the phone can be a great way to sell multiple product lines, build a strong business, and extract value by cross-selling to your existing customer base. You can do so by reducing the cost of marketing and all other expenses associated with selling your products and services face-to-face.

At Pantheon Technologies, one of my companies, we have managed to build a robust Health and Dental insurance business solely based on telesales.

In this chapter, we shall take a 30-thousand-foot view of the institution of telesales, its effectiveness and the kind of results one can expect to obtain when selling stuff over the phone.

## Numbers don't lie

*They sure don't.*

As mundane and sometimes intimidating as the idea of sales and telesales may seem, one cannot deny the effectiveness of using telephony technology as your main means by which you reach out to existing and potential customers to offer them products and services.

There are many reasons why any salesperson or entrepreneur will want to at the very least add phone sales as part of their overall marketing and sales initiatives.

Among many of the key performance indicators to be excited about, below are the ones one must first examine to determine if telesales is right for you.

## Healthy returns

*"Return on investment (ROI) measures the gain or loss generated on an investment relative to the amount of money invested.*

*ROI is usually expressed as a percentage and is typically used for personal financial decisions, to compare a company's profitability or to compare the efficiency of different investments."*

The issue of return on investment (ROI)when it comes to telesales is a complex one to navigate. This is mainly because the return on investment when overlaid against the profitability of your campaign(s) and company as a whole varies greatly based on the type of business you are in.

That being said, there are certain types of products and/or services that are just perfectly suited for telesales. These tend to be lower cost upfront and can be sold with very little resistance on the front end.

In the next chapters, I will delve a little deeper into these types of offerings that work best with telesales. For now, know that all things being equal, you stand to extract approximately a factor of 10x from your telesales operations. Of Course, success in telesales, like any other business endeavor will greatly depend on your level of consistency, time horizon (6 - 12 months), and a few other factors.

### *Example 1:*

A California insurance agency that wanted to expand its footprint in manufacturing invested $28,000 in a telesales campaign, which generated eight accounts and $239,875 in premium. An obviously healthy return of almost ten times their initial investment.

***Example 2:***

Another Insurance outfit spent $9,000 in telemarketing to target the construction industry. That investment garnered four accounts and $104,000 in premium.

## *Turning conversations into conversions*

How well do you and/or your sales folks convert? So, what am I talking about here? Let me start with a textbook definition of conversion rates as it relates to sales in general.

Your conversion rate will be simply defined as the percentage of folks who take the required action, i.e. make a purchase, sign up for a service, after and because of a conversation with a salesperson. Once again, conversion rates will vary greatly from product to product, marketing campaign to ... you get the picture.

But! generally, you can expect to get about 3 - 5 percent of the folks you talk to, with the right targeting, scripting, and offer, to convert. I will talk a bit about scripting in the coming chapters as well.

As far as targeting goes, you can either do some research to figure out who your ideal customer will be or glean that information from your existing customer data. These are the only types of folks you want to target; AKA get on the phone with.

## *Getting past the Gatekeepers*

If your product or services is meant to be sold to consumers, then you will almost never have this issue. What issue am I referring to? Navigating those that stand in your way of speaking to the person in the position to make a buying decision.

Sure, you will sometimes call to speak to a person and get a spouse or family member on the phone who will ask a few questions before handing the phone to your prospect, but this hardly happens. You will run into this issue more if you are selling to other business folks. Here you will more than likely talk to someone for whom making sure you do not get to this person unless you show obvious value, or you have some prior contact with the decision-maker is a big part of their job.

There are times when you will get the person you need on the phone immediately even in business-to-business (B2B) sales, but this will happen often if you are selling to very small companies or other solopreneurs like yourself.

More than likely, however, you will often run into Gatekeepers and your scripting must adjust for this issue. You will also want to track how often you get Gatekeepers on the phone and how often you are connected to the person you want. A higher percentage (not in your favor) could be a sign that something needs to be changed in your approach. So sure, you will have some Gatekeepers turn you away.

### # of calls made or received

Whether you set up an outbound calling apparatus or one that allows you to, as a result of some other kinds of marketing, take in-bound calls, you will want to keep an eye on how many calls you and your agents connect with or make.

This particular metric is a very important one to most sales folks for many reasons.

For starters, if you have a team of salespeople manning the phones at your company, keeping track of calls made and/or received will help you determine (with absolute precision) the productivity level of each agent.

You will get to know folks who play the call avoidance game, those who burn through opportunities needlessly without making an earnest effort to convert prospects and of course those that are efficient at making and/or taking a whole bunch of calls while maintaining a healthy conversion rate.

Armed with this granular data, you will be able to adjust your call or lead distribution strategy, making sure your best agents are placed in position to try to convert the opportunities on which you spend the most marketing dollars.

# ⇄ CHAPTER TWO⇄

# BEST LAID PLANS

### *Telesales is direct*

*Telesales, like any other type of marketing activity, is meant to put your products and services in the hands of your prospective customers.*

This is a similar idea behind social media marketing, face-to-face sales, email marketing and so on.

The main difference between phone sales and all these other marketing channels is that while the likes of social media and television advertising are meant to broadcast a message to as many potential candidates as possible, allowing your prospective customer, armed with all the information needed to either visit a brick-and-mortar or your online presence to initiate a transaction, Telesales, on the other hand, is direct.

### *True phone sales*

Salespeople, in most cases, make or receive these types of calls with the express intention of closing a sale. Often times, some sales organizations use phone sales as just a means to generate interest in their offering, only to allow either the initial agents or some other party to either invite the prospect to visit with them, or they themselves go to the company or individual to close a sale.

FYI, I do not consider the latter to be a telesales experience in the truest sense.

### *Three major questions*

When it comes down to it, the best telesales campaigns, the most successful ones, both in the short-term and long-term are ones that are planned well. Planning is everything when it comes to your phone sales campaign or any other business activity.

You want to build a coherent, replicable strategy. For your telesales campaign to work, you will have to answer three major questions.

*What will you sell?*

*How will you generate leads/prospective calls?*

*How will sales deals be closed?*

Most people reading this book, I am sure you have already answered the first question. But in the off chance that you haven't, if for some reason you have no idea what to sell, have no fear for I will discuss some telesales-ready products in the next few chapters. In this chapter, I will try to answer the last two questions.

### *So how do you get folks on the phone with you?*

Well, there are two main ways to get your prospective customers on the phone with you in order to try to make a sale. You can either call them, which seems pretty straightforward or get them to call you. Calling folks on the phone i.e. cold calling is a marketing activity as old as time. Most folks dislike cold calling, and I get it. It's an activity, not for the faint of heart.

It is oftentimes tedious, repetitive and seems to the untrained eye to yield very little results. I on the other hand find cold calling to be very profitable, that is if you are offering products that can be easily purchased over the phone and selling a recognized product type and/ or brand.

### *A dialing expedition*

Cold calling, however, can be just what your company needs to generate some low-cost sales. By low-cost, I mean that you will not have to spend a whole lot of marketing dollars to extract revenue from this type of outbound calling system. With cold calling, the key is to identify your customer profile, find a great source of leads and embark on a dialing expedition.

Of course, you will want to know what to say to folks when they answer the phone. For this reason, I will cover scripting and scripts in my next few chapters. The key to successful cold calling is creating large lead lists with precisely the information needed to identify and determine whether your leads are ideal prospects.

## *Leading with data*

There are many sources of leads out there, from companies that claim to do the marketing for you and provide you with the data you need, to companies that simply provide you with a large database of consumers and businesses to search using a plethora of geographic, demographic and psychographic filters.

And I know this can seem confusing to newer sales entrepreneurs. I get that. I was in a very similar position when I launched my first "real" company.

The key to finding a great lead source is to keep in mind that you will burn through most of these leads, no matter how accurate the provider is at finding folks that fit into your customer profile. You simply want to find a provider of low-cost leads with reasonably accurate information on their leads. Once you have obtained these leads from a firm like Listshack or Salesfully, (a company I own), you will be able to proceed with your outbound cold calling activities.

## In-bound maneuverings

For the purpose of this book, I want to focus more on how you can get your phone to ring with prospective customers on the other side ready to hear more about your offerings and perhaps make a purchase.

There is only one major way for this to happen, and that is, you need to put your offer out there, highlighting the features that will attract your ideal customer to want to take action, i.e. call to ask questions.

You will want to create various systems around which this happens. As I stated before, your first step in generating interest in your products is to create various ads to attract your ideal customer.

For the purpose of this section, I will assume that your organization or you are looking to generate phone calls from folks looking to hear more about or buy what you have to offer.

In this case, let's call that Life insurance or more specifically permanent life insurance sold to individuals. These are the types of policies, Like Whole life that you look into when you get to a certain age in life.

Let's say that since you are doing phone sales, you are not restricted by geography. So, we will want to know who you are targeting.

### long-term decision makers

### (Whole Life Scenario)

*Here, based on my years of experience, you are first looking to reach women as they are the decision-makers in any family, especially when it comes to financial matters concerning the well-being of members of the household.*

*You also want to reach her when she is above the age of 56 and thinking about retirement. By this time, she is starting to make some long-term decisions about her, and her husband's lives considering their advanced ages, financial standing, i.e. retirement savings, and so on.*

You want her to live outside of a major city. In other words, you do not want to reach out to savvy city-dwellers as they tend to seek financial advice from folks, they already have a relationship with.

Now, keep in mind that while local papers are great to place ads in to reach this type of prospect, these days, you will want to also launch a multi-pronged online campaign as well as avail yourself of low-cost mailing services like the USPS's Every door direct mail program.

### Every Door Direct Mail

Use Every Door Direct Mail® (EDDM®) services to promote your small business in your local community. If you're having a sale, opening a new location, or offering coupons, EDDM can help you send postcards, menus, and flyers to the right customers. Use the

*EDDM Online Tool to map ZIP Code(s)™ and neighborhoods—even filter by age, income, or household size1 using U.S. Census data.*

Based on data from Esi, here is what your customer looks like:

(Source: https://www.esri.com/library/brochures/tapestry-segmentation.pdf)

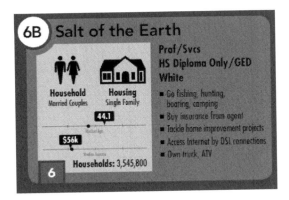

**6E Rural Resort Dwellers**

Svcs/Prof
College Degree
White

- Tend vegetable gardens
- Own low-risk assets
- Go hunting, freshwater fishing
- Watch National Geographic, Discovery Channel, Weather Channel
- Own older, domestic vehicles

Household
Married Couples w/No Kids

Housing
Single Fam/Seasonal
54.1

$50k

Households: 1,227,200

6

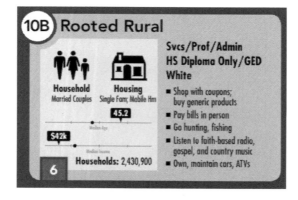

**10B Rooted Rural**

Svcs/Prof/Admin
HS Diploma Only/GED
White

- Shop with coupons; buy generic products
- Pay bills in person
- Go hunting, fishing
- Listen to faith-based radio, gospel, and country music
- Own, maintain cars, ATVs

Household
Married Couples

Housing
Single Fam; Mobile Hm
45.2

$42k

Households: 2,430,900

6

## *Platforms*

There are various major online destinations to utilize to try to reach the most viable candidates possible. In the past, I have found success targeting this particular group on Facebook, and via the use of Google Ads to help attract eyeballs, and ultimately calls from my ideal prospect.

Both tools give you the ability to precisely target the types of folks you want to see your ads in any part of the world. This is why I find both to be extremely effective. There are several other factors that contribute to a successful campaign of course.

Your work is far from done. You will, sure, want to target folks that are the most likely to buy what you sell, but you will also want to speak directly to them using every part of your ad.

Both Google and Facebook have a similar ad structure which makes it a bit easier to illustrate which parts of your ads you will want to ensure speak directly to your prospects.

## *Facebook Ad components*

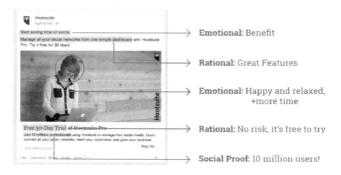

## *Messaging*

Success in any sales and marketing scenario is heavily reliant on patience and the basic structure of your ads themselves. Messaging is paramount here.

You will want your ads to employ graphics, videos, and text that speak directly to the needs and wants of your ideal prospective customers.

Your messaging should use all available emotional and psychological tools to motivate your prospect to take the desired action.

Which in this case is to call you.

Please note that your messaging doesn't just start and end with the actual text of your ads. Nope, your ads' message should be incorporated into every part of your ad.

Your graphics, sound, text format, etc. All should convey the message you are trying to put out there.

## General text

The general text, the meat of your ad should speak to your prospects using various terms and phrases that inspire or motivate them to want to call you.

## Features and benefits

Features are generally the "what" your products and services can do for your customers. Features are basically a general list of what your product does.

For example, any basic feature list of a Smartphone will go a little something like this: 1) You can make and receive calls. 2) You can surf the internet and use various apps. You get the picture.

Benefits, however, speak to the features that matter the most to your prospect. The features that will make a difference in their unique circumstances.

A mother of three young boys cares about nothing else other than the fact that the minivan she is looking to purchase has stain-proof interior upholstery and that she can drive her boys back and forth to soccer practice and school, and whatever else kids do these days. Nothing else really matters to her.

Not the Horsepower, 0-60 in god knows how many seconds, none of that.

The well-understood rule about sales is to play to the benefits in each sales interaction based on the type of prospect you are talking to at the time.

Keep in mind that here, your online ads as well your newspaper and radio ads will all count as sales interactions, so you will want to use the same rules.

## Sense of urgency

This is pretty self-explanatory.
You will want to, without seeming too pushy, create a sense of urgency around your sales interactions/offer.

You want your prospects to get the sense that "this opportunity won't last ".
Most humans need some sense of urgency to help us make decisions.

This is the reason why even though we can at any time during the month pay our rent, we all wait till the end of the month to do so.

We wait until we absolutely have to do things to do them.

Not all things, just the ones we find boring or perceive as more of a "have to" than a "want to"

## *"Call me now for a free tarot reading"*

In my Miss. Cleo voice. Say what you want about her, she did have a very simple and powerful call to action. One that is still stuck in my head twenty-something years later. If you are under the age of 35 reading this book and have no idea what I am talking about then stop reading for a second and look up "Miss Cleo" on YouTube.

Why YouTube? Because you have to see her in video to appreciate the tour de force that she was with those late-night ads.

Calls-to-action (CTA's) are very vital to the success of your campaign. These are the simple, yet powerful statements at the end of any ad that tells the prospect what to do next.

In this scenario, your call-to-action is pretty straightforward. You want to tell folks to "Call you for more information". You will also want to remind folks of your offer even in your call-to-action. Geico, Warren Buffett's insurance outfit does a great job at this - "Geico, a 15-minute call could save you 15% on car insurance". Here, the company even includes that call to action and benefits in their tagline.

## ⇄ CHAPTER THREE⇄

## CODE RED

***Red Ventures!***

If you are not familiar with them, Red Ventures is a Fort Mill, South Carolina marketing outfit that specializes in the resale of communications and technology services and products to consumers.

To me, they are the best at what they do. They have built a reputable brand and infrastructure that fully engages the true essence of a direct-to-consumer marketing telesales operation.

I once worked for them a while ago, and I gained a whole new perspective for what it means to deliver results via telesales.

I went on to build my various businesses, using skills picked up while I was employed by them.

### *Telco's and more*

The company has a strict set of criteria a product must meet to be able to fit into their view of what they can sell.

In the next chapter, I will delve a bit into what I think, in my experience features a product must have in order for it to be easily sold via telephone sales. The company, Red Ventures also had a pretty extensive list of what a product or service needs to look like in order for it to be marketed by their thousand-plus salesforce.

My supervisor at the time told me that in order for RV to sell a product or service, it must:

*Must require no cash upfront from the customer during the sale.*

*Must be a non-physical product or service. So here we are talking about internet service, Insurance products, Streaming services, etc.*

## Google Ads

Red Ventures primarily generates sales leads via various online advertising campaigns. They lean on Google Ads to generate most of their inbound calling traffic. The company takes this very seriously.

They use well-designed online landing pages, packed with specific language and calls-to-action to entice prospective customers to call their various toll-free numbers to speak to a sales agent.

*They generate their leads with a set up that goes like this:*

*Sales operation*

Once a prospective customer calls in, as sales

**Google Ad**

**Landing page**

**Sales agents**

agents, we were armed with various tools to help the customer take the action we required.

I worked on the Verizon Fios team. This meant that my goal when prospects called in was to help explain the various service levels, the features and the benefits of each of Verizon's Internet and premium cable offerings.

The company provided dynamic scripts to help answer any questions the prospect may have and to strategically walk them through signing up for the service. One package or the other, what "signing up" meant was to set up an appointment for Verizon agents to go out to the prospect's home or place of business to perform a service install, only then would the prospect have actually become a customer. This was when, as a sales agent, I got paid a commission.

Other service offerings also involved setting up an account for customers to receive accessories, add-on services, and more. Our sales operation was a very well-run, numbers-oriented one. The company relies heavily on statistical data to gauge the effectiveness of their operations and to know when changes are required.

Verizon Fios Customized TV Packages | 877-688-2032
https://fios.verizon.com › fios-tv ▾
Select from a variety of channels and **package** options to build your **Fios** TV plan. ... **Price.**
$69.99/mo*. Plan Name. **Fios** Gigabit Connection & Custom **TV.**

# Verizon Fios ( s | 877-688-2032

https://fios.verizc ; to build your **Fios TV** plan

Select from a variet ustom **TV**.

$69.99/mo*. Plan N

The starting point of every sales interaction when it comes to Red Venture's Verizon Fios team is their online Google Ads, search ads to be exact.

Here the company uses compelling

language right in their ads and even gives folks some pricing info and the number to call, right there in the body of their Google Ads.

Verizon Fios Landing page

## *Pricing Data*

Providing pricing data in your ads is a very effective tool if you are, a) confident you have the best prices on the market, and b) if that is your main selling point.

If that is the biggest difference between you and your competitors.

Showing your prices in your ads or

giving folks a taste of what it costs to go with your product or service will be a great way to help attract immediate attention.

⇄ CHAPTER FOUR⇄

**TELE-READY**

So now that we have somewhat fully covered various pertinent aspects of telesales and how you can employ this kind of prospect outreach vehicle, it's time, I think, to take a look at some of the kinds of products and services that work well when sold over the phone.

## My shortlist

As I have stated before, I am by no means suggesting that there cannot be a more extend list or set of features that would allow other kinds of offering to be sold over the phone. I am in no way the foremost authority on this subject matter.

Truth is, if you can sell something in person or online, then you can conceivably sell it over the phone.

There are, however, some types of offerings that just work very well when sold over the phone. That is all I am saying. I am rather going to list the various features that in my experience make an item or service ideal for telesales.

## *Frictionless*

In my opinion, the most important rule or call it "feature" that any product being sold over the phone or in any other channel must possess is the "easy to sign up " factor. This is numero uno in my book. This is especially true if you are offering discretionary products or services with lots of competitors.

Think about it, we take our time when we visit the Doctor's office to fill out those lengthy forms for two reasons: 1) Our lives may depend on providing accurate information to the Doctor and her staff, and 2) Well, we need medical help.

Now imagine if Kohls started handing

out long forms for customers to fill out as a requirement to shop at their stores. What do you think folks will do? They will shop elsewhere. Right? If your product is not a " need to have" product and has lots of competing products on the market, then the first thing you want to do, especially as it relates to telesales is to make it very easy to get started as a customer.

You can learn quite a bit from the software-as-a-service outfits. Firms like FreshBooks, Salesforce, and Slack make it super easy to get started using their online software applications. Some kind of risk-free trial is key to getting as many folks to try the service as possible.

All these firms require just an email address and your name to get started. Once you are on-board, they will give you more reasons to pay for the service. Keep this strategy in mind as you plan to roll out your own product(s) and your telesales operation to help market it.

## *Products mentioned:*

- *Software -as-a-service platforms*

## *No money upfront*

Keeping in-line with the idea of making your products and services frictionless, and I touched a bit on this topic earlier, taking no cash upfront from users is a very powerful tool.

Consumers feel in control when they make purchases this way. Again, here, this is really powerful if you are, say selling a contact management system. The internet is crowded with various firms selling these types of CRM products.

Now granted, each has its own unique features. The thing is folks can't tell if they don't get to use it first. Allowing your prospects to get to test your product risk-free is one great way to beat out the competition without breaking the bank paying for advertising. And in case you are wondering, which I am sure you are, this type of strategy also works with physical products.

***Especially products that are a pain for the prospective customer to return.***

So, think, exercise equipment, Residential and commercial alarm systems, automobiles, lawn and garden hardware, home entertainment systems, etc. *Pelaton*, the fancy workout hardware provider employs this kind of strategy to help get their products in the homes of their prospective customers. They now offer a 30-day risk-free trial on their high-tech stationary bikes.

## Products mentioned:

- *Exercise equipment*

- *Lawn and garden hardware*

- *Home entertainment systems*

- *Computer hardware*

- *Kitchen equipment*

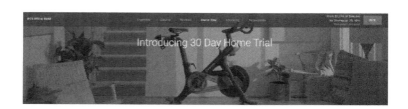

Try the Bike for yourself at home

*Pelaton (https://www.onepeloton.com/)*

### Virtual

This is a pretty straightforward idea. Although, not a steadfast rule. Yes, you can sell physical products over the phone. Sure, you will have to set up a logistics/shipping and delivery system to go with your phone sales.

That is, of course, doable and has been done for many years.

Because however, shipping costs can be a pain - *Walmart does not make any money with their eCommerce business due to high shipping costs*, I always recommend to smaller startups to try as much as possible to stick to virtual products at least until you figure out how to navigate telesales and your business as a whole.

### Strong brand

A strong brand can go a long way in getting

folks to pay attention. If you are thinking about what kinds of products to sell over the phone, and you are not looking to create your own products and/or services, this is a great opportunity for you.

What I am trying to say is that you are in a great position to pick which company's services or products you want to represent.

Unless you come up with some kind of side deal where you can gain an equity position as a result of your sales agreement Like Lebron James did with Beats by Dre.

It is reported that James agreed to wear and also get his teammates to wear the now-famous headphones during the Olympics, thus providing global exposure for a brand that up until then was struggling to gain momentum, in exchange for a small stake in the company. An equity position that according to The Washington Post netted Lebron about $30 million. The NBA superstar was able to cash-in on this agreement when the headphone maker was sold to Apple in 2014 for $3 billion.

On the other hand, you can just decide to sell products and services that already have a strong brand and goodwill. Like in the previous example with Red Ventures and Verizon Fios. Here RV relies on the strong brand Verizon possesses to help sell their entertainment and data packages.

Most Financial Advisors and insurance professionals are able to easily recommend products to their clients based on various partnerships they hold with well-known insurance companies, banks, asset management firms, etc.

## *Defined audience*

I believe that no matter what you plan to sell or how you plan to sell it. Whether over the phone, online, or face-to-face, you need to know exactly who the audience for your product is.

It does not matter what you are selling, even when selling yourself to potential life partners or dates. Anyone can be "a catch", as long as you know who you are more likely to be a catch to. Your dating life could be a very exciting one if you just play to your audience.

Such is the case in sales and marketing. Taking your time to research and establish your defined audience will help with your advertising strategy, kind of language used in your scripting, pricing, and so much more.

Now, if you do not have the resources to do the research to define your audience, then your best bet is to only sell products with a well-defined audience.

If you were to decide to become a reseller of reverse mortgage solutions, you would immediately have a very good idea as to what your audience will be. There is no "anyone will want this " type of product.

Not even medical services. Sure, we all get sick and need medical assistance from time to time, but some of us, for one reason or the other just don't seek medical services unless it is an emergency.

In this case, you would assume incorrectly if you deduced that "anyone" would be a great candidate for Health insurance.

# ⇄ CHAPTER FIVE⇄

# SOME BEAUTIFUL PITCHES

A script is essentially a well-thought-out roadmap designed to help navigate any pitfalls that may arise during a salesperson's interactions with customers, clients and/or prospective clients.

This is my take on the definition of what a sales script essentially is.

In this chapter, we shall take a look at a handful of telesales scripts. These examples are merely meant to give you some ideas on how to generate your own product-specific sales scripts.

### *Let's talk about scripts*

In any sales scenario, you will want to know what to say, how to say it, and when to say it.

In fact, no self-respecting sales professional leaves any part of their sales presentation or any conversation with a prospective customer to chance. One of the many issues I had when I first launched my insurance sales company was scripting.

We (my wife and I) built from scratch various sales scripts. We created scripts for phone sales when we were pitching a product for the first time.

We made scripts that would walk our agents and us through every step of an in-person appointment with a potential client, and many more. As I said, we made scripts for almost every possible sales scenario in our business.

We quickly realized how easy,

having these readily available scripts made managing our clients. Our agents, regardless of how long they had been with us, always had guides ready to help them get through, with success, their sales calls. Our entire team was on the same page as a result of having company-wide sales scripts.

## Scripts matter

An investment in the development of quality custom sales scripts is one of the most important ones you will ever make as far as your telesales system goes. For many reasons, having quality scripts your team can use when talking to prospects and customers can help streamline your business and increase your sales numbers. Some of the reasons to develop uniform scripts for your team to use include:

## Tongue-tied

Let's be honest, sales in and of itself is not natural. I know there are some folks who swear they are natural-born sales folks but that is a bunch of malarkey.

No one likes to talk to random strangers about their products and services. Especially in outbound telesales. No one, and I mean, no one likes to call up strangers to chat with them about a product or service.

We do it because when done correctly can be very lucrative but, nobody actually enjoys sales. Well... not the prospecting part anyway, which is the most important part.

We all get a bit nervous during our first interactions with a prospective client, and when we get nervous, we all from time to time ran out of things to say. Or worse, say the wrong things. Having sales scripts available, even for more experienced sales professionals can help outsource the "what to say" part so we focus (in the conversation) on closing the deal.

### *Rapport-building*

They say, "People buy from people they like, period" and I believe this to be true. In all my years of sales, I have never witnessed anyone buy a product or service from someone or a company they hated. We only do so when we have no other options. Sure, companies like Duke Energy and Comcast have seen to it that they are the only choice in their service areas, but this is hardly the case in other types of services.

Living in a capitalist country, that is hardly the case. There are about a gillion different options for any product category.

Walmart alone has over 30 different kinds of butter for sale, from 15 different brands. Getting your prospects to like you from a professional standpoint is essential even in telesales. Having complete scripts chocked full of information to help answer any questions a prospective customer may have will go a long way to help build rapport between your customers and your team.

## Lead-generation

Scripts are great at helping generate quality leads for your firm. How? Even when a sale is not made on a call, having and using an information-riddled script will help generate genuine interest on the part of your prospect, making it easier to follow up with them at a later date and time.

Once you initiate the second call, due to the fact that they got all the information they needed on the first call, they, the prospect will be armed with all the pertinent information they need to take the next step.

### *A few Good scripts*

The following are some of my favorite scripts out there on the interwebs. Remember, these examples are just meant to help serve as a guide to you while you work to create your very own set of scripts for your telesales operation.

### *Sample Script for a First-Time Call*

*Source:([https://callhub.io/telemarketing-script/](https://callhub.io/telemarketing-script/))*

*Introduction: Hello Joel, this is Scott calling from Zirg Pro. I hope you're having a nice day. Can I talk to you for a few minutes?*

*Connecting Statement: Great! I've had an eye on Net Ventures for a while now and I saw you closed a big round of funding last month. Congrats on that!*

*Pitch: The purpose of my call is to let you know that our business helps companies optimize their websites to improve the amount of traffic they're bringing in regularly. I would like to make sure that we're on the same page, so I'd just like to ask you a couple of questions if you don't mind, Joel.*

*Pre-qualifiers: Fantastic. Okay, so currently:*

*– Are you getting as much traffic to your site as you'd like?*

*– Are your customers happy with your site functionality?*

*Sample Problems(Optional): Since Zirg Pro has a relationship with several businesses such as Phoenix and The Smart Inc amongst others, some of the common challenges that they face are a poor conversion rate or a website layout which customers find difficult to navigate. Do any these problems sound familiar to you?*

*Proposed Benefits: So as I mentioned before, our company provides website optimization services while enhancing the user experience of your site. We help drive more traffic to your site and improve site functionality so that customers quickly find what they want helping boost your conversion rate.*

*We've consistently been ranked among the top 10 web optimization companies by the US Business Tech Awards and we have decades of experience in enhancing customer satisfaction.*

*Ask: I know you've probably got a busy schedule, but I'd love to book a slot this week to have one of our consultants walk you through our product. Would this Thursday, 5 pm work for you?*

*Awesome! I'll book a slot and send a confirmation email right away. It was great talking to you, Joel!*

### Sample Script when talking to Prospect's Secretary/Gatekeeper

*Source:([https://callhub.io/telemarketing-script/](https://callhub.io/telemarketing-script/))*

*Good morning/afternoon sir/ma'am. I'm Scott calling from Zirg Pro. Am I speaking with {prospect's name}?*

*If Yes, follow above script. If No, i.e. you're talking with a gatekeeper, continue.*

*Our business helps companies optimize their websites to improve the amount of traffic they're bringing in regularly. I would like to schedule a call with {prospect name} to talk more about the services we offer.*

*If they aren't interested:*

*Oh, that's too bad. Can I have {prospect's name} email id/contact number so that I'd be able to directly contact them? Thank you.*

*If the prospect is unavailable:*

*Oh, that's no worry. Can you tell me when {prospect name} would be free so I can contact them at a later time when it's convenient? Thanks for your assistance.*

*If they offer to transfer, you to voicemail:*

*That's alright, is there someone else I could talk to? {try getting connected to another person with a similar job profile as your prospect}*

*If they give contact details of the prospect:*

*Great! I'll be sure to contact {prospect}. Thanks for helping. Goodbye!*

## Sample Script: Talent and recruiting services

*Source:(* https://blog.hubspot.com/sales/sales-scripts-examples*)*

**Salesperson:** *"Hello, [Prospect name]. My name is Michael Halper and I help hiring managers like you reduce the time it takes to interview, hire, and onboard new talent in 50% less time than the industry average. How many new hires do you have planned for the year?"*

**Prospect:** "Well, my department has the budget for seven new hires in 2019."

**Salesperson:** "What's your biggest pain point in the hiring process right now?"

**Prospect:** "I've got a million other things going on and finding qualified candidates has been a challenge. We need to get these positions filled, but I'm having a hard time making it a priority with everything else on my plate."

**Salesperson:** "I hear that a lot. I'd love to set up a 10-minute call to learn more about your goals this year and share how Recruiters International might be able to help. What about this Thursday?"

**Prospect:** *"Um, sure. I think I've got an 11:00 open."*

### Sample Script, Introduction: Talent and recruiting services

*Source:(* <https://blog.hubspot.com/sales/sales-scripts-examples>*)*

*"Hello [prospect's name], this is Michael Halper from Recruiters International. Have I caught you in the middle of anything?"*

**Value Statement**

*"Great. The purpose of my call is that we help hiring managers to:"*

*[Insert your value points here]*

**(Optional) Disqualify Statement**

*"I actually don't know if you are a good fit for what we provide so I just had a question or two."*

*(pause or ask for agreement or availability)* If you have a couple of minutes?

## Pre-Qualifying Questions

*"If I could ask you quickly:"*

*[Insert your questions here]*

## Examples of Common Problems

*"Oh, OK. Well, as we talk with other hiring managers, we have noticed they often say:"*

*[Insert your pain points here]*

*"Are any of those areas you are concerned about?"*

## Company and Product Info

*"Based on what you have shared, it might productive for us to talk in more detail."*

*"As I said, I am with Recruiters International and we provide:"*

*[Insert some brief details about product, service, and/or company]*

**Close**

*"But since I have called you out of the blue, I do not want to take any more of your time to talk right now."*

*"You have asked some good questions and there is a little more information that I would like to share. I would also like to learn more about you. Are you available for a 15-20 minute meeting where we can discuss your goals and challenges and share some examples of how we have helped other managers build top-caliber teams?"*

# ⇄ CHAPTER SIX⇄

## RESOURCES

### *Tools to get the job done*

Every salesperson, entrepreneur, etc. Looking to generate new sales opportunities via telesales needs to not only be armed with skills and knowledge, but also the right tools to get the job done.

In your quest to dominate phone sales

and take your company's profitability to new heights, you will come to rely heavily on software platforms to perform most of the tasks we have talked about here in this book.

Every time I author one of these technical, how-to books, I try to make sure that the reader has all the pertinent information needed to access some of the tools I mention in my books. So here are links, data ( provided by each individual company) and resources to access the various tools mentioned in this book and more.

## Sales (data) leads

*Salesfully*
www.salesfully.com

## Overview

Salesfully is the best software platform for generating unlimited b2b or consumer sales leads. Our platform houses Over 200 million U.S.A Consumer and business sales leads.

*Infofree*

*www.infofree.com*

*Overview*

Unlimited Sales Leads, Business Profiles, Person Search & Contact Manager. Only $99/month for 2 users, additional users $49/month... No Contract, Cancel anytime

*Listshack*

*www.listshack.com*

## Overview

Our mission is simple: to help salespeople, marketers, and small businesses get more clients. We do this by providing a comprehensive database of sales leads available 24 hours a day, seven days a week, with the filters you need.

## Customer profiling

### Esri: Tapestry

https://www.esri.com/en-us/arcgis/products/tapestry-segmentation/overview

*Overview*

Understand customers' lifestyle choices, what they buy, and how they spend their free time. Tapestry gives you insights to help you identify your best customers, optimal sites, and underserved markets. As a result, you will get higher response rates, avoid less profitable areas, and invest your resources more wisely.

*Mosaic by Experien*

http://www.experian.com/marketing-services/mosaicportal.html

*Overview*

Experian Marketing Services' Mosaic USA is a household-based consumer lifestyle segmentation that empowers marketers with the insights needed to anticipate the behavior, attitudes and preferences of their most profitable customers and reach them in the most effective channels with the best messages.

## Sales scripts

*Sales Scripter*

https://salesscripter.com/

*Overview*

Sales Scripter is an all-in-one sales automation platform that provides:

- Call Scripts
- Prospecting Email Templates
- Objection Responses
- Voicemail Scripts
- CRM
- Email Automation
- Lead Scoring Analytics

- Gamification

*Scriptly*

https://www.scriptly.me/

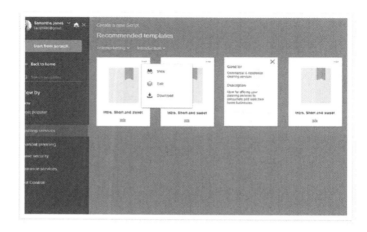

*Overview*

Find and fully customize highly-rated sales scripts.

## **Direct Mail services**

*USPS Every Door Direct Mail*

*Overview*

Use Every Door Direct Mail® (EDDM®) services to promote your small business in your local community. If you're having a sale, opening a new location, or offering coupons, EDDM can help you send postcards, menus, and flyers to the right customers. Use the EDDM Online Tool to map ZIP Code(s)™ and neighborhoods—even filter by age, income, or household size1 using U.S. Census data.

*Vistaprint direct mail*

https://www.vistaprint.com/marketing-materials/postcard-mailing-services/templates?msv=true&rd=1

## Overview

Time is money – and you'll save both with Postcard Mailing services. Enter your mailing preferences below and see how inexpensive it is.

# ABOUT THE AUTHOR

Frank is a serial entrepreneur and hobbyist. Over the last ten years, he, along with his wife and business partner, Bernice has founded and run various businesses.

The couple started out by starting an independent insurance agency. A business they still own and operate. Their agency opened its doors in 2011. The same year they met.

The company was initially started by Frank. Bernice soon joined as a partner. They grew the company into a profitable venture and later started Corvus (www.corvus.website), a software business that was started as a way for them to build software solutions for their insurance business.

Soon, other businesses were subscribing to what has become numerous software applications.

The couple is currently investors and partners in various other business ventures. They spend most of their time in Charlotte, North Carolina, where they live. Frank is originally from Ghana, West Africa where he was born and raised till he moved to Philadelphia, Pennsylvania. Frank has always had an entrepreneurial spirit. Seeing his father build, along with his mother, the family business.

He always wanted to start his own company, and soon did after college and a few years in the corporate world. Today, Frank spends his time running his business and writing business and sales books whenever he gets some free time.

He has, till date published over six business books. All his books can be purchased at www.ostrichpress.com or on Amazon.com.

**AUTHOR'S OTHER BOOKS**

### *Adventures in Marketing Automation*

https://www.amazon.com/dp/1696291518

## *Overview*

Adventures in Marketing Automation is a simple but comprehensive guide on how any small business owner or entrepreneur can use the power of social media, email, SMS, and other tools to help automate their entire marketing systems. All in an effort to grow a more efficient and profitable business.

*The Social Media Handbook: Harness the power of Social media to grow your small business*

## *Overview*

IN EVERY CHAPTER OF this book, I will share with you, based on my own experience, dozens of practical ideas, tips, and insights that will set you on the path to harnessing the awesome power of social media to grow your business. I will introduce you to the history of social media, the current state of social media, and try to share some thoughts on how to set up your very own Social media campaigns. You will learn about the latest social media platforms out there, and how to use these platforms to find new customers for your products and services.

**PIXIE DUST: How to Convince Investors to Invest in Your Business**

### Overview

This is an opportunity to learn how to attract investors to your business. Learn how to position yourself and your company or business idea to attract Angel Investors and/ or Venture Capital investors.

*Recurring Revenue: A Practical Guide to help you launch your very own Software-as-a-service business*

## *Overview*

Recurring Revenue Provides any aspiring tech entrepreneur with an easy-to-follow roadmap on how to plan, build and market a Software-as-a-service application. In this book, I share my tips and lessons learned from my years of experience starting and running a 100%

subscription-based software services firm. I provide some information on what makes a "Good" app idea, how to build it and ways to market it and get folks to sign up.

**Email Marketing in A Digital Age: Learn how to attract new customers**

*through the power of Email Marketing and Social Media*

https://www.amazon.com/dp/B07VLTXF8Z

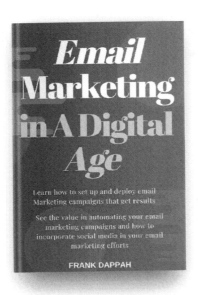

## Overview

Email Marketing in A Digital Age is a simple, easy-to-read guide on Email marketing. This 150-page book will guide any small business owner or entrepreneur through the process of setting up and deploying effective email marketing campaigns.

# THE
# TELESALES
# HANDBOOK

## Learn How to Sell Anything Over the Phone

### FRANK DAPPAH

*Co-Founder of Corvus Web Services*
*www.corvus.website*

# THE
# TELESALES
# HANDBOOK

## Learn How to Sell Anything
## Over the Phone

## FRANK DAPPAH

*Co-Founder of Corvus Web Services*
*www.corvus.website*

## Ostrich Publishers

*Charlotte, NC 28212*

Copyright © 2020 by Frank Dappah

Ostrich Publishers is an ardent supporter and facilitator of creativity and the free flow of communication. We aim to inspire and help bring to the public quality literary works of independent Authors around the world. Thank you for buying an authorized edition of this book and complying with copyright laws by not reproducing, scanning or distributing any part of it in any form without permission. You are supporting writers and allowing Ostrich to have the resources to continue to publish books for everyone.

ISBN: 9781673465327

For more information about products and services or perhaps to make additional purchases, visit our official website at www.ostrichpress.com. We look forward to producing and /or publishing more books in the future. You can also visit Amazon.com or anywhere books are sold to purchase any of our other works.

# THE
# TELESALES
# HANDBOOK

## Learn How to Sell Anything
## Over the Phone

## FRANK DAPPAH

*Co-Founder of Corvus Web Services*
*www.corvus.website*